Seasonally Defective

A Collection of Poetry and Musings for Goddesses and Mortal Women

ALY SEBASTIAN

ISBN: 0692570144
ISBN-13: 978-0692570142

For my Daughter

CONTENTS

<u>She calls and I answer</u>

She Calls and I Answer

She has come crashing down around my feet
And beckoned "Become water."
And I became changeable.
Waiting placidly or raging like a torrent
Ebbing and flowing according to the moon's
command

She has ignited me
And dared "Become fire!"
And I burned fiercely
Wild and dancing freely
Smoldering with heat and passion

I heard Her whisper on a breeze
Enticing me "Become Air"
And I was carried off

Gusting playfully through hill and dale
Going wherever inspiration took me

She has stopped me in my tracks
And demanded "Be like Earth."
And I dug in deeply
I rooted myself to the spot
And gathered seeds and nurtured

Now I ask her
"What now shall I be?"
And She answers "I have already given you all
of my gifts."
Take up your torch and Chalice
And let the air keep your fire lit.
May the ground remain steady beneath your
feet as you walk."

I understand
I take up my gifts and I walk
I plant my seeds and water them from my cup
I warm them with my fire
And I watch myself grow toward Spirit

Systers Dance

Stomp your feet my syster
And I will stomp mine too
I will feel the earth tremble
As I stomp along with you

Shake the rattle syster
And I will bend my ear
I will hear it crackle on the wind
Like a whisper in my ear

Chant your chant my syster
And I will lend my voice
I will meld my words along with yours
For me there is no choice

Beat the drum my sister
And I will feel your beat
I will feel it in my bones
and tap it with my feet

Cry the cry my syster
And I will echo every cry
I will call across the distance
And my voice will soar and fly

Poetry for Goddesses and Mortal Women

Stir the pot my syster
And I will tend the fire
I will feed the flames and pinch the salt
And see it bubble ever higher

Sing the song my syster
And I will hum aloud the song
I'll hear your melody in my mind
And I will sing along

Dance the dance my syster
And I will sway along and dance
My feet will move in time with yours
As I spin and twirl and prance

No matter where you are my syster
I will feel you in my heart
I will hear you in my dreams
Even if we are apart

So shake the rattle syster
And sing and call and cry
And stir the pot and sing out loud
and dream and chant, stomp and fly
And remember dear syster
I am with you at all times

__Casting a Circle__

I cast a circle
flowing out from deep within
circling me in pale blue flame
power
I see it stretching before me
growing out to spread for miles and miles
hours and days
I see the joined hands of my grandmothers
my mother my daughter
my systers
I see it encompassing all which I love
all that is
will be

Poetry for Goddesses and Mortal Women

I see faces new and dear
long forgotten
smiling
Making it grow making it stretch
forming a perfect ring of light
and hope and love
protection
Illuminating the room the night
the house the sky
my soul
I see the circle going on and on
girdling the earth
embracing her
I feel it stretching out from my heart and soul
Flowering from my blood my womb
my breath
Spinning stretching dancing out on and on
unbreakable and unbroken
eternal

Winter

Life gives way to death and seasons change
The beauty that once was just a distant memory
now
The world grows colder and we all grow older
Making skeletons of trees of people
The frost seeks to form cracks in that which is
unbreakable
Even the light of the sun is scarce
We all scurry in search of warmth wherever
Finding solace in fond remembrances grown
faint
Icy winds touch our necks like the cold fingers

of death
Reminding us how frail and fleeting it all is
But still we continue on
Hoping once more for the spring of our youths
For that time when all is vibrant and alive
The world of the living that we had begun to
forget
And then it happens as if by sheer chance
A snowflake floats down from the sky like an
angel
Its perfection and intricacy aweing to the senses
Dazzling us with the fact that it is completely
unique
Formed like no other as we ourselves
Bringing back the light of past joys to rest
deeply within
That warms the soul and reaffirms that this too
is life
And as it melts it releases the smell of
childhood

I Am Like Water

I am the sea
Turbulent and deep
Embracing those who rest in my arms
Eternal and beautiful

And I am a boat
Strong and buoyant
Floating along the surface
Charting my own course

Poetry for Goddesses and Mortal Women

I am an ocean
The size of me cannot be measured
Untamed and untouched
A world beneath the surface

And I am the whale
Magnificent and gentle
Speaking only in song to those who listen
A majestic and loving creature

I am like a wave
Constantly seeking
Dancing with the earth
Destroying that which harms her

And I am the sand
Soft and beautiful
Capturing heat and holding it dear
Sparkling and timeless

I am the tide
Ebbing and flowing
Connected to all women
Sisters in the moonlight

And I am the moon
Shining down mysterious silver
Guiding those in darkness
The symbol of the goddess

I am a river
A raging torrent
Carving my own path
Building upon myself

And I am a gull
Gliding on the breeze
Feasting with relish
Flying away from danger

I am a lake
Placid on the surface
Teaming with life beneath
Warm and welcoming to all

And I am a willow
Arms wide to all
Solid and sturdy and withstanding
Growing always greater

I am the rain
Cool and refreshing
Nurturing the earth
Leaving beauty in my wake

And I am the rose
Wild and sweet
A gift for all the world
Synonymous with love

Poetry for Goddesses and Mortal Women

I am like water
The cradle of life
That what quenches all thirsts
And washes all clean

And I am a person
Adrift in that sea
Swimming in that ocean
Fighting that tide
Riding that wave
And becoming that water

UNVARNISHED/TARNISHED

I have grown weary of trying
To smooth away all of my rough edges.
Trying to fit in a mold that I am malformed for.
Feeling I am not good enough.
As I am.
Too crass. Too Vulgar. Too Poor. Too Rough.
Too Real.
Too willing to let my roots show.
Unapologetic for the circumstances I was born
to.
The polish keeps cracking.
I keep lacking.
I keep trying.
Trying to be who you want me to be.
I'm too smart to be so stupid.
I'm far to pretty to be sad
Or broken.
If I just keep working at it
I can become.
Just like everyone else.
Normal.
And then you will love me
For me.

<u>Untitled</u>

I feel like I'm being pushed as I stand against
the edge of the rabbit hole.

I don't know how not to fall.

<u>Text to Myself</u>

Wtf. Again I feel like this. I am not going to cry. I will not back down. I would rather be perceived as a bitch than treated like a child. What else can I do? I feel unimportant and that is bullshit. I am important. I mean a lot to people even if not to him. Someone can tell you that you mean the world to them but they may be the same people who litter and dump toxic waste and shit. Just sayin.

I've Waited Long Enough

Torrents of time wash over me

Eroding the layers of life I have put before you

I have stood in the same spot waiting

And the floor beneath me has rotted away

I plummet deeper into the chasm in my heart

Freefalling into darkness

Hoping I land on my feet

Praying I do not fall forever

That Which No Longer Serves
(I Too Grip the Past Tightly)

Some people hide behind their stories like a
child behind their favorite blanket who then
brings that wubby forward into adulthood. The
familiarity of the thing is a strange comfort and
even though it's outgrown and tattered and
filthy they hang on tight. Even when it leaves
them exposed and cold.

Fool

Destruction follows you like a shadow
Broken hearts cast aside like discarded
eggshells
Broken promises not spoken aloud
Shattered lives
Vows of flesh and whispered nothings
A doomed soldier thinking only of conquest
Ignoring carnage left behind at home
Never looking back
Playing a game you can never win
With stakes too high and others left paying
Giving nothing but illusion
The truth a bloody stain
Can you live like this forever?
Ignoring tears wetting lips that speak your name
Before you know it, it will be too late
Callousness cannot be undone
Lies cannot be untold
And you will realize that it wasn't my heart you
broke
But your own

Past

a gift so easily given

stolen by a conniver

taken with consent but wrapped in a coating of

lies

nothing left to do but say thank you

an innocent offer blind to all consequence

the driving need of the thief to take

to replace what was lost so long ago it is all but

Poetry for Goddesses and Mortal Women

forgotten

a hunger that can only be appeased by blood

no promises

a hurt so deep in a bruised heart

hidden beneath naiveté

salty sweat burns wounds long unhealed

left to fester awaiting sweet relief

of honeyed words that hide putrification

sadism is a state of mind

hurt mixed with love mixed with glory

mixed feelings of discontent

disconnected from reality

from the fantasy you wish to see

I am the monster

and I will devour you

why do you let me

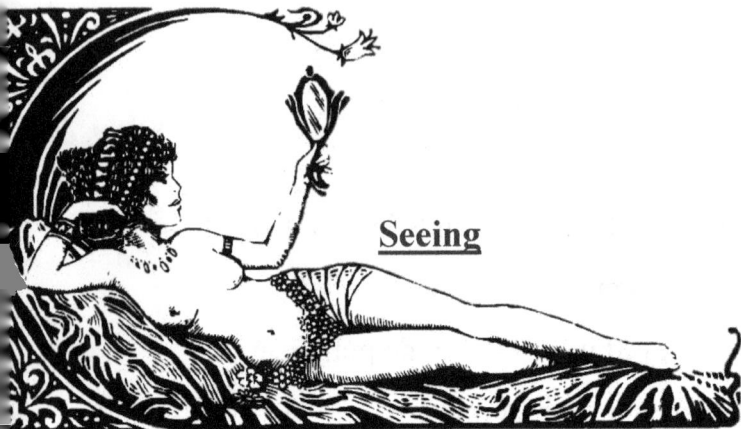

<u>Seeing</u>

Shattered reflection staring back

Through bruised iris unwithered

Glassy pools deeply empty

Seeing only in remembrances

Blindly finding light in shadows

Frozen in timelessness

Waiting

Poetry for Goddesses and Mortal Women

<u>Phoenix</u>

High I soar above the clouds
Gliding wherever the wind takes me
Uncaring of the danger that surrounds
My wild and careless flight

Many times I have died
At the hands of hunters wishing to possess me
To hold that which should be free
That should remain forever wild

A million deaths I have suffered

At cruel and gentle hands both
That trapped and tried to take
The very essence of my being

From the ashes I have risen
From flames that sought to consume me
But only made me stronger
I rise and soar to new heights

Kill me they cannot
And have me they shall never
I am a creature of magick
Whose spirit refuses to be killed

So point your arrow at my heart
Watch my freefall to the earth
And when you claim my burning body
I will fly away once more

Poetry for Goddesses and Mortal Women

<u>Lament for Spring</u>

Artemis aim your arrow and let fly
It is time again for The Stag to die
Shoot for his heart in his glen in the wood
Color the flowers once more with his blood
His time is over and it's now time for you
to make the world again warm and fragrant and
new
I know it will break your heart to kill your old
friend
As you must do year after year, again and again
But Artemis raise once again your bow
And awaken the Earth beneath the snow
You are the Huntress and this is your fate
Winter is ending and Spring cannot wait

Suspended Animation

 I stand here with my feet encased in ice and
wait
Frozen in this place of death and cold as is my
fate

Unable to move freely, bound here as Hel
I would even welcome the fires of Muspell!

Oh Ivaldi! Release me! So I may be Idhunn
once more!
I call out to you Arvakr, Alsvid, And Sol! Your
light I adore!

I am weary and saddened and trapped and my
Sleetden is cold
and I have grown weary and wish to cross
Gjoll!

I can see the colors of Bifrost in the distance
and I pine

Poetry for Goddesses and Mortal Women

to return to Asgard and my youth I've been
denied!

This time of men and darkness must end
so I may walk through Asgard and return to my
Vingolf again

My Valkyries please fly me away from this
place!
Imbolc is coming there's no time to waste!

I must become Idunn filled with glorious
warmth and sweet light
and to bid farewell once again to Nott's endless
night

So Release me Ivaldi and light the fires of
Spring!
End my lament! Return me to the world of the
Living!

<u>Mother</u>

oh mother, what have we done to you
we have sliced open your womb
and left you to bleed all alone
endlessly
painfully
oh mother, I can't stop the tears
or the pain I feel in reflection
throbbing deep in my center
endlessly

seeringly
oh mother, what can I do for you
how can I save you
when I am but one
I can only weep for you
endlessly
woefully
oh mother, please, how can I heal you
shall I will swim into your arms
and let my blood mix with yours
endlessly
hopefully
oh mother I will give you my strength
and my blood and my tears
my love and my wishes
endlessly
lovingly
oh mother, I am your child
I cannot stand by and watch
I can't see you hurting
endlessly
endlessly

Scent of Promise

Through painful ache of shivered bones
Through barest boughs of creaky moans
Through withered skin of wise old crones
I smell spring.

Through wailing winds of winter's throes
Through tingled skin of frosted toes
Through crimson cheek and pinkened nose
I smell spring.

Through splintered ice of frozen roads
Through tempestuous flurries riotously strowed
Through silvered clouds of burdensome loads
I smell spring.

Through light of hearth and candle glow
Through circling flight of hungry crow
Through all of this one fact I know
I smell spring

The Garden of Our Souls

I think of the word Soul it brings to mind the
word Soil.
Fertile earth in which to plant and grow things.
The stuff in which
all life is created and the stuff in which all
things return.

Our souls are like soil. I like to think of it as a
garden, since no
soul is completely fallow. Every soul is born
with its own garden, a
reflection of itself in earthly form. Some say the
soul is the
garden.

When we are babies our Mothers and fathers
tend this garden for us,
watering it, putting up fences or walls, letting

sunshine in, tending
to weeds, and often planting seeds of their choosing. Hopefully they
also teach us how to properly care for this garden so that we may
learn to do so ourselves when we are able.

When we are small children we let everyone in to play in our garden.
Wildflowers bloom everywhere and the sun shines constantly and we let
the rain water our tenacious buds without a care.

When we get a little older and become teenagers we gain even more
control over our garden. We begin to plant our own seeds and we begin
to build our own walls but the gate remains open. With our open gate
policy though, not only does it let in friends, but also lets in
other things to nibble away at our roots and eat away at our fruits.
Nature and our parents still help to tend to our garden though and
usually no permanent damage is done.

When we become adults we have the full responsibility of tending our
garden. The seeds sown throughout our lives are

either in full bloom
or long since withered away, unable to grow in
the climate we've
created. Some grow fruit and vegetation that
will sustain them
throughout their lives. Some have grown trees
to shade them and
protect them from the elements and give them
shade and sometimes a
place to climb high and view the heavens. Some
plant flowers of
different hues and sweet scents to forever
surround themselves with
beauty. Everyone's garden is special and
individual and ever growing.

Unfortunately, we do not always remember the
daily task of nurturing
our gardens. We sometimes skip days, weeks,
even years and hope that
nature will take care of it for us. Walls become
weakened, weeds take
hold, our beautiful blooms wilt, and things
begin to die. We forget
the task of tending this treasure. We forget that
we must give it
light, which we get from knowledge and
wisdom, fertilizer that we
make from love, and rain which comes from our

tears. We have children
that we don't realize get their very seeds they'll use in their
gardens from our own, and that if we don't remember how to be
gardeners we cannot teach them the same. We must tend to the garden
of our souls daily. We must plant and prune and help it grow strong.
We are all from the same earth but we must plant what we want to see
in our futures today. We must not let our gardens wilt away and
become barren and cold. Tend to your garden and tend to your soul and
you can make the world a more beautiful place.

I Write

I write to become real.

I write for myself because the rest of the world isn't real to me.

Only in the work I create do I exist as a whole and not a ghost.

I write to become real.

To make real the place where I hide.

Behind every turn of phrase and every evoked vision.

I mask myself in the faces of others that I was too scared to be more than a stranger to.

I shrink back from them and disappear into myself

while some other person takes possession of my words and spouts banalities.

I uncloak myself again and again on pages unending but new worlds keep popping up.

Even as I battle them with a pen as my sword and nudity my armor.

I write for myself.

Because my story needs to be told no matter how scattered and diluted.

I will draw a map of myself and strew it across books

So that when I need to, I can find myself again.

And if by chance someone else is looking,

they and find me there within the pages and finally someone can say,

"I know her."

Daughter

You should love your beauty

But know only the inside counts

You should be positive always

But cry or rage when you need

You should be daring and brave

But always willing to ask for help

You should be healthy and strong

But know how to indulge on occasion

You should be passionate

But know how to be at peace

You should be intelligent

But look to the world with curiosity

You should be successful

But never forget your roots

You should be kind to others

But don't let others walk all over you

You should be…

Whatever the fuck you want to

And I love you for who you are

Poetry for Goddesses and Mortal Women

The Womb of Sadness

(Seasonally Defective)

I have survived another winter

By going inward to hibernate

In the dark cave of rumination

Pretending candles are the sun

I have survived the icing over

Of my heart's fiery passion

Tears of diamonds

Frozen on numbed flesh

I have survived the torment

Of the never-ending snowfall

Buried in sadness and regret

Rewriting my past by moonlight

And wishing upon stars

Yes!

I have survived even as I've died

Spring is now upon me

And I rejoice in my rebirth

From the womb of sadness

SEASONALLY DEFECTIVE

Poetry for Goddesses and Mortal Women

ABOUT THE AUTHOR

Aly is a writer and an artist. She works in the metaphysical field and uses that mysterious world and her unique perspective to enrich her writing. She lives in Massachusetts with her husband and three wonderful children.